T0207591

Living a Life You Love

A Workbook for a Richer, More Beautiful Life

Diane S. Brissey, LCSWC

BALBOA.PRESS
A DIVISION OF HAY HOUSE

Balboa Press books may be ordered through booksellers or by contacting:

Balboa Press
A Division of Hay House
1663 Liberty Drive
Bloomington, IN 47403
www.balboapress.com
844-682-1282

ISBN: 978-1-9822-5961-7 (sc)
ISBN: 978-1-9822-5962-4 (e)

Library of Congress Control Number: 2020923880

Print information available on the last page.

Balboa Press rev. date: 08/03/2021

Contents

Introduction

Over the years working as a therapist, focusing on my own growth as well as that of countless others, I have been able to identify factors that both hinder and help our path to wellness. I have come to believe that having an overall wellness plan is the key to overcoming today's mental health issues, health crisis, and our own drive for fulfillment in our lives. In 2018, I created Acadia Counseling and Wellness, which would become a wellness community focused on all aspects of health and wellness. I am excited to continue that journey by creating this workbook for those who may not be able to engage personally with our services. I hope to share with you at least a portion of what we provide to our clients so that you too can begin—or perhaps continue—your journey to personal wellness.

At this moment, you may be experiencing problems with a family member, struggling with a feeling of depression, or just questioning your purpose in this life. I will identify eight aspects of wellness that I believe we all need to focus on in order to feel complete, whole, and fulfilled.

By honestly evaluating and improving your life in each of these areas, you will be able to more accurately identify where you are struggling and need improvement and where you excel. Throughout this workbook, I would like to challenge you to unleash your potential by identifying your personal goals and dreams as well as the obstacles that you allow to get in your way. I will help you to evaluate where you are now in each of these areas and develop a plan to get you to where you want to be. Please don't see this as a one-time event in your life. I would encourage you to, at least once a year, reevaluate yourself in all areas, as our needs, goals, and desires continue to change over time.

It's so easy to get caught up in the day-to-day that you stop focusing on where you want to put your energy and instead just go through the motions with no real plan or goal in mind. It's that day-to-day rut when at some point you stop to question, "Am I really moving forward with what's important to me?" Oftentimes, I encounter clients who do not have a clear destination in mind when asked what they want to create for themselves. Without a goal in mind, it is all but impossible to hit the target. You too may feel stuck and be unsure about what you need to do to change your situation. As a result, you may be devoting time and energy to routines, problems, or tasks that do not bring you any closer to your destination. Together, we will renew our commitment to ourselves and to those who are most important in our lives. You will take charge of your life, feel energized, and become intentional in your day-to-day interactions.

Throughout this workbook, you will find a menu of items that can be used to improve your overall wellness. Your job is to pick and choose those items that are right for you. As I stated before, this is not a "fix it and forget it" type of workbook. Hopefully, you will use it year after year to reflect on where you are and where you want to be. As our lives change and we grow, so do our priorities, our hopes, and our dreams. As we reach one destination, we look ahead to see what is next. Consider this the first step on a lifelong path of growth and self-discovery.

Wellness reflects how one feels about life as well as one's ability to function effectively in all areas.

Ten Tenets of Wellness

1) Happiness is a choice.
2) Good health isn't a gift; it is a decision you make every day.
3) A healthy, fit body is not enough; true fitness also encompasses your emotions and spirit.
4) Practice gratitude daily.
5) Learn to laugh and do it often.
6) Nurture your spirit; it is a source of love and strength.
7) Stay connected to the natural world; it will nourish and enrich your spirit.
8) Believe in yourself; you have been given everything you need.
9) It's never too late to take the first step.
10) Where you put your attention is what will thrive. Choose wisely.

The first step to achieving wellness is to identify where you are right now. To take a realistic look at what areas you are rocking and which you may be ignoring, take a few minutes and complete the questionnaire that follows. Once you have taken an honest look at where you are, you will pick one area—or possibly two—that you would like to focus on. This could be your weakest area or maybe the one you deem most important in your life right now. Here goes. Have fun!

Chapter 1

Assessment

Dimension 1: Physical Wellness

For each question, please rate where you are currently, using the following key:

1—rarely, if ever   2—sometimes   3—most of the time   4—always

_____ 1) I maintain a desirable weight.

_____ 2) I engage in aerobic exercise, such as brisk walking, two to five hours a week.

_____ 3) I do strength-based exercises two to three times a week.

_____ 4) I get enough sleep at night to wake up on my own in the morning feeling refreshed.

_____ 5) My immune system is strong, and I am able to avoid getting sick.

_____ 6) My body heals itself quickly when I do get sick or injured.

_____ 7) I do not smoke.

_____ 8) I do not abuse alcohol or binge drink.

_____ 9) I have lots of energy and can get through the day without being overly tired.

_____ 10) I eat a nutritious and well-balanced diet.

_____ 11) I avoid highly refined and processed foods.

_____ 12) While eating for wellness, I am aware of extremes and careful of absolutes.

_____ 13) I grow some of my own food or obtain it from a local source.

_____ 14) I am aware that my nutritional needs are unique, and I attempt to learn what I can about how best to meet my body's own requirements.

Dimension 2: Social Wellness

For each question, please rate where you are currently, using the following key:

1—rarely, if ever   2—sometimes   3—most of the time   4—always

_____ 1) I am able to assert myself when necessary.

_____ 2) I am open, honest, and get along well with others

_____ 3) I acknowledge and apologize for any mistakes I make instead of trying to cover them up.

_____ 4) I am aware of my behaviors that have caused problems in my interactions with others.

_____ 5) I feel good about the degree of closeness I have with the people in my life.

_____ 6) I am a good listener.

_____ 7) I am open and accessible to a loving and responsible relationship.

_____ 8) I have someone I can talk to about my private feelings.

_____ 9) I consider how what I say may be perceived by others before I speak.

_____ 10) I have a person in my life who I enjoy spending time with.

_____ 11) I am able to listen to and objectively consider opposing viewpoints.

_____ 12) I clearly express my thoughts and feelings instead of assuming others can read my mind.

_____ 13) I spend more time with the people I care about than I do engaging in social media.

_____ 14) I feel that I am part of a community.

Dimension 3: Emotional Wellness

For each question, please rate where you are currently, using the following key:

1—rarely, if ever   2—sometimes   3—most of the time   4—always

_____ 1) I avoid using drugs or alcohol as a means of coping with problems.

_____ 2) When I am angry, I try to let others know in a nonconfrontational and nonhurtful way.

_____ 3) I feel optimistic about the direction my life is going.

_____ 4) I take responsibility for my own feelings and behaviors.

_____ 5) My moods are generally stable.

_____ 6) I recognize when I am stressed and take steps to relax through exercise, quiet time, or other activities.

_____ 7) I feel good about myself.

_____ 8) When I am upset, I talk to others and actively try to work through my problem.

_____ 9) I am flexible and adapt to change in a positive way.

_____ 10) I enjoy receiving compliments and recognition from others.

_____ 11) I enjoy giving appreciation and recognition to others.

_____ 12) I am able to say no to people without feeling guilty.

_____ 13) I ask for help when needed.

_____ 14) I am aware that my feelings provide me with information about myself and use them to further my growth and evolution.

Dimension 4: Environmental Wellness

For each question, please rate where you are currently. using the following key:

1—rarely, if ever   2—sometimes   3—most of the time   4—always

_____ 1) I enjoy spending time outside in natural settings.

_____ 2) I recycle.

_____ 3) I try to buy products that are recyclable.

_____ 4) I try not to leave the faucet running too long when I brush my teeth or shave.

_____ 5) I am aware of environmental issues.

_____ 6) I take steps to conserve energy.

_____ 7) My physical environment is comfortable and relaxing.

_____ 8) I am aware of the changing seasons and attune my body's responses to different temperatures, hours of daylight, and so on.

_____ 9) I grow some of my own foods.

_____ 10) I am aware of which foods are best to eat.

_____ 11) I avoid environmental toxins.

_____ 12) My home is not cluttered.

_____ 13) I do not expose myself to secondhand smoke.

_____ 14) I avoid exposure to sprays, chemical fumes, and exhaust gas.

Dimension 5: Spiritual Wellness

For each question, please rate where you are currently, using the following key:

1—rarely, if ever   2—sometimes   3—most of the time   4—always

_____ 1) I believe my life has direction and meaning.

_____ 2) I believe life is a precious gift that should be nurtured.

_____ 3) I take time alone to think about what is important in life—who I am, what I value, where I fit in, and where I'm going.

_____ 4) I engage in acts of caring and goodwill without expecting anything.

_____ 5) I feel empathy for those who are suffering and try to help them through difficult times.

_____ 6) I feel confident that I have touched the lives of others in a positive way.

_____ 7) I work for peace in my interpersonal relationships and my community.

_____ 8) I go for the gusto and experience life to the fullest.

_____ 9) I regularly experience feelings of gratitude.

_____ 10) I take time to enjoy nature and the beauty around me.

_____ 11) I balance the challenges and stresses of my life with playful and nurturing attitudes and activities.

_____ 12) I live my life with the knowledge that I have within me everything that I need for my happiness.

_____ 13) I meditate or practice some kind of relaxation or centering process.

_____ 14) I set realistic goals that support me manifesting my dreams and aspirations.

Dimension 6: Financial Wellness

For each question, please rate where you are currently, using the following key:
1—rarely, if ever   2—sometimes   3—most of the time   4—always

_____ 1) I feel in control of my personal finances.

_____ 2) I have a budget and know where my money goes each month.

_____ 3) I avoid the use of credit cards.

_____ 4) I avoid impulse buying and do not use shopping as a form of recreation.

_____ 5) I have a three- to six-month emergency fund established that is either fully funded or I am savings toward.

_____ 6) I save at least 10 percent of my income each month.

_____ 7) I do not carry debt through loans or credit cards.

_____ 8) My partner and I agree on financial decisions so as not to create a source of stress between us.

_____ 9) I regularly compare prices on my purchases and monthly expenditures.

_____ 10) I have both short-term and long-term financial goals.

_____ 11) I am investing in my retirement.

_____ 12) I know money is important but do not make it more important than spending time with people I love.

_____ 13) I am able to balance my checking account monthly.

_____ 14) I help others through donations on a regular basis.

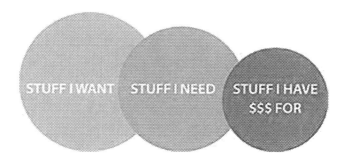

Dimension 7: Occupational Wellness

For each question, please rate where you are currently, using the following key:

1—rarely, if ever   2—sometimes   3—most of the time   4—always

_____ 1) I have identified my career interests, skills, and abilities.

_____ 2) I have a good idea of how marriage, family, and career fit together.

_____ 3) I have set occupational goals for myself.

_____ 4) I enjoy going to work most days.

_____ 5) I have a manageable workload.

_____ 6) I feel I can talk to my boss and coworkers when problems arise.

_____ 7) The work I do is rewarding for me.

_____ 8) I am proud of my accomplishments.

_____ 9) My job responsibilities and duties are consistent with my values.

_____ 10) My job contributes positively to my overall well-being.

_____ 11) I have positive relationships with coworkers.

_____ 12) I have energy left at the end of my workday for other activities.

_____ 13) I find my work to be motivating and interesting most days.

_____ 14) I feel I am able to use my talents and gifts in the work I do.

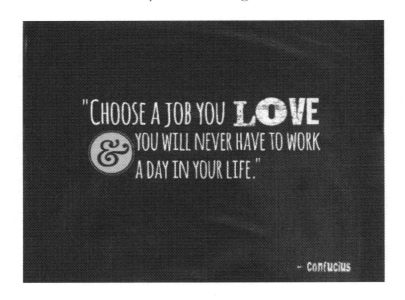

Dimension 8: Intellectual Wellness

For each question, please rate where you are currently, using the following key:
1—rarely, if ever   2—sometimes   3—most of the time   4—always

_____ 1) I am able to effectively schedule my time.

_____ 2) I feel capable of making important decisions.

_____ 3) I know how to set and reach goals and objectives.

_____ 4) I have read a nonfiction book in the last six months.

_____ 5) I can identify at least one thing I would like to learn more about.

_____ 6) I am open to new ideas.

_____ 7) I look for ways to use my creativity.

_____ 8) I search for learning opportunities and stimulating mental activities.

_____ 9) My life is exciting and challenging.

_____ 10) I recognize that the responsibility for my health and wellness lies with me rather than with others.

_____ 11) It is easy for me to pay attention, focus, and concentrate when needed.

_____ 12) I am able to solve problems by creative methods (i.e., brainstorming, journaling, etc.).

_____ 13) I approach life with the attitude that no problem is too big to solve.

_____ 14) I initiate conversations.

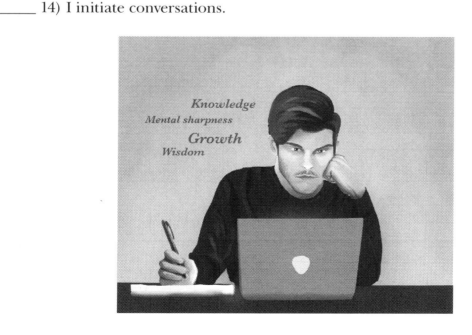

RESULTS

Physical: _____/56_

Social: _____/56_

Emotional: _____/56_

Environmental: _____/56_

Spiritual: _____/56_

Financial: _____/56_

Occupational: _____/56_

Intellectual: _____/56_

44–56: This is a strength for you. You spend time ensuring wellness in this area.

35–43: This area needs some improvement. Set at least one goal in the areas with this score to improve your overall wellness.

Below 34: This is an area that is deficient and could be impacting your overall wellness. Spend some time deciding what changes you could make in this area and set short-term and long-term goals. Life coaching or counseling may be beneficial.

You should now have a better understanding of where you are on all eight dimensions. Take a few minutes and think about your results. Are they what you expected? Are there areas that you had previously not considered? Were there any surprises? As you decide where you want to make changes in your life and what areas of growth are most important to you, take a minute and answer these questions.

What in my life brings me joy right now?

_____

_____

_____

_____

_____

What do I want to learn over the next several months or year?

_____

_____

_____

_____

_____

If nothing could hold me back, what would I take on, attempt, or go for in my life?

_____

_____

_____

_____

_____

Who means the most to me, and how do I show them?

_____

_____

_____

_____

_____

You will use your responses to these as you move forward in this workbook and begin setting goals for yourself. For now, pick one section you would like to begin working on and proceed to that part of the workbook.

Chapter 2

Physical Wellness

What Is Physical Wellness?

This is perhaps one of the most important areas you will address in your journey to wellness. We have all experienced times when we weren't feeling well physically, whether from a short-term illness or a lack of self-care. Let's be honest: when you don't feel good in your body, it's difficult to focus on anything else in your life. So if this is an area that you know you need to improve, congratulations—it will make an enormous difference in your life overall.

Physical wellness is the maintenance of a healthy body through good nutrition, regular movement, and the avoidance of harmful habits. The physical benefits include having more energy, better health, and improved sleep. The psychological benefits to physical wellness include enhanced self-esteem, a more positive outlook on life, and a sense of direction. To begin, I want you to answer a few questions:

1) What do you know you should do that you are not doing in regard to your physical health?

   _____

2) What do you know you should not do that you are doing in regard to your physical health?

   _____

3) Most importantly, why do you want to make a change in this area? How do you want to look and feel differently?

   _____

Barriers to Getting Healthy

It's important to identify what has been holding you back from achieving your goals. Everyone is different and has their own barriers to change, but generally speaking, there are two main types of barriers to change: internal and external barriers.

Internal Barriers

These barriers take the form of negative self-talk and limiting beliefs—stories such as "No matter how hard I try, I can't lose weight," "I hate exercising; I'm no good at it," and "My parents were fat and riddled with health problems; so were my grandparents, and so are my siblings, so, of course, I am too."

First, you need to identify what outside events or messages planted this belief in you. Perhaps being picked on during gym class led to an aversion to any sort of team sport or fitness endeavor. Perhaps you binge ate because your parents forced you to finish every morsel on your plate, even when you were stuffed beyond capacity.

It may become clear that you use food to self-medicate or sabotage your wellness efforts by not exercising. By understanding your thoughts and beliefs around food and movement, you can better create an individualized wellness program.

Take a moment and write down your beliefs around food. Is food used as a means of celebration and how you express joy? Do you believe that it's rude not to eat something that is offered to you? Was food offered to you whenever you were sad or disappointed to comfort you? Write down whatever you experienced and what you feel is true for you.

Second, acknowledge the ways you have repeated and held onto these beliefs throughout your life. Things happened in the past, but they have no more significance than what is happening literally right this second. The past only has the power we give it each day. How would your life change for the better if you were able to change these beliefs around food to serve you better?

- What do you need to let go of?
- What needs to take its place?
- What life do you really want to be living?
- What beliefs do you truly want to ascribe to, apart from other people's or society's expectations?

It takes time to retrain the brain. The new messages may not ring true for a while. This doesn't matter. Here are some tangible ways you can learn to embrace these new beliefs.

Ten minutes of visualization a day. Visualize the life you desire. Be specific. How will you look? How will your body feel? How will you carry yourself differently? What choices will you make daily around nutrition and exercise? How do you feel, having made these changes in your life? Living in that feeling for ten minutes each day is a powerful motivator for change!

Make a solid commitment. You must be committed, both to the health plan you develop and to the new beliefs. Whenever a negative belief starts running through your mind, replace it with the more positive one you've created. So, when the voice in your head chimes in with *I don't know why I'm even trying. I'm always going to be fat*, send it on its way and replace it with a more positive affirmation, such as *I feel better, and my body is responding to the positive changes I'm making*. Most importantly, remind yourself why these changes are important to you.

Likewise, keep track of your accomplishments, big and small, and create a list of events you'd like to participate in. Then pick dates to do the items on the list. For instance, make a list of things you'd like to do instead of eating compulsively or sitting on the couch after work and put that list somewhere you can see it daily. Commit to one endeavor from that list every week.

Affirmations and mantras. Affirmations and mantras are a part of basic brain functioning. For something to get lodged in your brain, it has to be grounded in either the shock of major trauma or the consistency of daily input. An affirmation, mantra, personal saying, or whatever you want to call it is totally meaningless said once or twice or even ten times. The ultimate point is you can't just say it—you have to mean it! Say it out loud. Throw your shoulders back, hold your head up high, and say it with confidence.

Here are some to get you started:

- Every day, in every way, I am getting healthier and stronger.
- All the cells in my body are returning to their perfect original blueprint.
- I am energetic, vigorous, and full of health and vitality.
- Every action I take moves me toward improved health.
- I am a perfect example of fitness and health.

Cultivate belief. A key element to internal change is belief. If you believe you can make a change, you're much more likely to actually have success in making that change happen. If you merely want or hope for change, you will ultimately feel incapable of accepting or sticking to the necessary behaviors and will sabotage yourself from the start.

You must believe that you have what it takes to show up for yourself on a daily basis, to accomplish the task you've set out to complete, and to let the momentum take you to levels of health you desperately want or maybe can't even envision yet.

External Barriers

Here are a few examples of external barriers you may face, along with solutions to overcoming them.

Lack of support. As personal as a commitment to health is, there's always a social dimension. You may have a noticeably different approach to healthy living than your family and friends do, and you may stumble upon some uncomfortable situations and conversations.

Perhaps a friend or family member's resistance emerges not because they are concerned so much about your health progress but because the changes being made are causing them to reflect on their own health choices or lack thereof, and that makes them uncomfortable. Where possible, increase your support for healthy eating by including your family and friends in choosing or preparing meals. Invite family members or friends to join you for a walk or bike ride.

Conventional wisdom. Conventional wisdom is a lumbering beast: slow to move but difficult to alter course. Our standard American diet is outdated but continues to be espoused, which can cause confusion. You must find the approach that works for you. I often suggest an elimination diet as a great way to identify those foods that affect you negatively. I will talk more about that in a little bit.

The top five things to take away:

1. **Every day, you manage your health—regardless of your intent.**

   It's a critical realization: whether we have a plan or not, what we do each day influences our health one way or another. Every choice is an input that the body uses to function. How well it can function is based on those exact choices.

   What you feed your body, how much you move, how much rest you get, how much stress you subject yourself to—it's all input for the body, and every day, you are the gatekeeper.

2. **Just get started … and keep going.**

   If you were to wait for the perfect circumstances to begin new healthy behaviors (or any new choice), the fact is you would never begin. The complications of life will always be there for you to contend with, so the answer to "When do I start?" is *today*!

   It's simply about doing something different, making one choice at a time. Getting started is committing this moment to something healthier, to something better. You aren't claiming to be a more disciplined or motivated person. You're simply choosing one thing over another to the benefit of yourself. Then you do it again. You keep going, regardless of whether you feel like it or not. You do it because you know where it will take you.

3. **The way you talk to yourself has consequences for your success.**

"Why do I always screw up every time I try to watch what I eat?" "I'm not an athlete." "I thrive off of stress." "I'm destined to be heavy." "I'm not a high-energy person."

Reclaiming health often means recalibrating your identity as well as your behaviors. What have you come to believe about yourself over the years? The fact is what you tell yourself is out of reach will likely remain so until you decide (and speak) differently. So be mindful of the words you choose and create a more positive mind-set.

4. **Your process won't look like other people's, and it shouldn't.**

Many people believe there's a set formula they should be able to follow—a universal answer they can easily take up without much fuss or thought on their part. "Just tell me what to do," we often say. You have to be ready not only to show up but also to fully own your process.

To own your process means to personalize it, to shape basic health principles and practices to your own interests, lifestyle, and personality. To be sustainable, a health program needs to fit your needs and preferences. If you are more introverted and desire quiet and space, exercising outdoors rather than at a gym might be a better choice. On the other hand, you may feel more motivated working out in group classes and run clubs. If you have unusual work or parenting schedules, you might choose to time meals differently or employ fasting practices.

5. **Cultivating health is a long-term endeavor.**

As the old adage goes, Rome wasn't built in a day, and neither is our health. We build it, in fact, one day at a time, one choice at a time. Although individual goals give us something to aim for, our overarching purpose should be living healthy, vibrant lives across the full span of our years. This will inevitably be a labor of love and a lifelong evolution at that. You have time—time to lose the fat you want, time to build strength, time to gain the resilience to climb mountains or keep up with the grandkids, time to move into the life you want. When you can accept health as a lifelong commitment, you will be able to see it as an act of continual creation. In doing so, you will likely learn the value of patience. Not everything will happen right away, and it's okay.

Choosing to live a healthy life means enjoying vitality today in whatever way it's available to you. It means having something to look forward to and achievements to celebrate, yet it also means accepting the process as a long arc toward self-actualization throughout the phases of life. Well-being will creatively shift and reveal itself over time if you stay committed to the greater purpose of living the healthiest life you can.

Nutrition

We won't go too in depth into the area of nutrition, as there are a lot of resources available, but I do want to give you the basics of an elimination diet. I believe that unless you undertake a short-term elimination process, it can be difficult to know how specific foods affect your mood and health. The purpose is to stop consuming anything that could be causing you distress in the form of bloating, heaviness, inflammation, fatigue, depression, or anxiety. After a brief period of elimination, I suggest twenty-one days, then slowly add the other foods back in one at a time to see how you feel. This will allow you to better understand what foods your body responds well to and what foods it does not. If this sounds like something you want to try, here are the basics.

- Eliminate bread, cereals, baked goods, and anything made from grains, whole or otherwise.
- Eliminate packaged and processed foods.
- Eliminate heavily processed seed, grain, and vegetable oils, such as corn oil, vegetable oil, safflower oil, and dressings.
- Eliminate sweet sugary drinks.
- Eliminate any dairy products.
- Don't worry about portions or calories. Other than those foods listed above, eat what you want, when you want.
- After the twenty-one-day period, begin by adding back dairy for the first week. Make this the only addition for that week and see how you feel. Do you know any difference in terms of digestion, joint pain, or bloating?
- The following week, add back whole grains and again notice any differences in how you feel or your energy levels throughout the day.
- It is not recommended that you add back the processed dressings and oils or sweets to your diet. These have long-term health ramifications and should not be part of your health plan.
- That said, try to live by the 80/20 rule. Once you have established what works for you, stick to those foods 80 percent of the time. Strict diet rules and lack of flexibility does not add to your overall wellness.

If a full elimination plan is not for you, then perhaps you are the type that likes to make slow, gradual changes over time. Start by making one specific change each week in the food choices that you make. I would suggest first eliminating hydrogenated seed and vegetable oils and dressings such as corn oil, vegetable oil, and safflower oil. Instead, use coconut oil, avocado oil, or olive oil, to name a few. This is the most significant change you can make, as these oils are tied to a large number of health issues. Although this may seem initially easy, be sure to read labels for any processed foods you buy, as these oils are often found in processed and packaged foods.

The following week, eliminate sugars and baked goods from your diet, again being sure to read labels to see where it may be showing up unexpectedly. For example, the majority of jarred spaghetti sauces have added sugar, and barbecue sauces often contain high-fructose corn syrup, so read thoroughly before making your choice.

Continue in this manner, each week eliminating a food that you know is not healthy for you. The following is a food pyramid that I recommend as being the basis for your overall diet plan, taking it one step at a time. This pyramid was originally developed by Mark Sisson, who developed the Primal Blueprint. You can find more information at www.marksdailyapple.com.

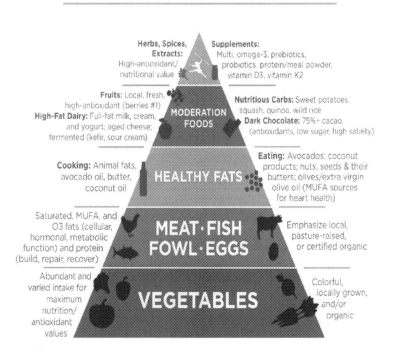

THE PRIMAL BLUEPRINT FOOD PYRAMID

- Nutritious, satisfying, high-nutrient-value, low-insulin-stimulating foods.
- Low carbohydrate, moderate protein, ample nutritious fats.
- Flexible choices and meal habits by personal preference.
- Free of grains, sugars, and refined vegetable oils.

Herbs, Spices, Extracts: High-antioxidant/ nutritional value

Supplements: Multi, omega-3, prebiotics, probiotics, protein/meal powder, vitamin D3, vitamin K2

Fruits: Local, fresh, high-antioxidant (berries #1)
High-Fat Dairy: Full-fat milk, cream, and yogurt; aged cheese; fermented (kefir, sour cream)

MODERATION FOODS

Nutritious Carbs: Sweet potatoes, squash, quinoa, wild rice
Dark Chocolate: 75%+ cacao, (antioxidants, low sugar, high satiety)

Cooking: Animal fats, avocado oil, butter, coconut oil

HEALTHY FATS

Eating: Avocados; coconut products; nuts, seeds & their butters; olives/extra virgin olive oil (MUFA sources for heart health)

Saturated, MUFA, and O3 fats (cellular, hormonal, metabolic function) and protein (build, repair, recover)

MEAT·FISH FOWL·EGGS

Emphasize local, pasture-raised, or certified organic

Abundant and varied intake for maximum nutrition/ antioxidant values

VEGETABLES

Colorful, locally grown, and/or organic

Movement

The second key component of improving your physical health is movement. Again, this is an area where there is a lot of information available, and where you start will be based on your overall fitness level. In general, the key is to move more, whether that's walking, riding a bike, taking the steps, or joining a class. You also need a combination of resistance exercises (weights or bodyweight), aerobic exercise, and interval movements, which vary in intensity. Primary resistance exercises include squats, push-ups, pull-ups, and planks. Again, depending on your current level of fitness, these moves can be made easier or more difficult. Here is a pyramid related to exercise showing where you should spend most of your time, which again is from the *Primal Blueprint* by Mark Sisson.

The nutrition and movement suggestions are based on a primal lifestyle. For more information, you may want to visit www.marksdailyapple.com or www.robbwolfe.com.

Chapter 3

Social Wellness

What Is Social Wellness?

Social wellness encompasses many areas of your life. It is the ability to perform social roles, establish and maintain friendships, and feel comfortable interacting with others under various situations. It involves being a part of your community in whatever way works for you and attending activities that bring you joy and fulfillment. Yes, some people prefer to interact with others on a daily basis, while others may prefer more time alone. Either way, we are inherently made to be social.

To improve in the area of social wellness, it is important to do the following:

- recognize your own needs
- know how to communicate these needs
- be able to connect with other people who nurture these needs
- create a supportive network
- find a place where you can share similar interests with others

Connecting with Others

So, how will social wellness impact your life? As social beings, we interact every day with others. Some areas in which our lifestyle reflects our interactions are as follows:

- the types of interactions we have with others (positive versus negative)
- the amount of enjoyment we gain from these interactions
- the type of friendships we develop
- the ability to practice empathy
- our ability to care for others
- our ability to allow others to care for us

Let's begin by looking at a few of these core areas. First, do you plan time to be with family and friends? Do you make this a priority in your life? Write down what you enjoy doing with family and friends currently and what you would like to have more of in your life in this area.

_____
_____
_____
_____
_____
_____
_____

Second, do you enjoy the time you spend with others? Are you part of a group in your community? Do you have a hobby that you share with others? What has brought you joy in your life in the past six months in this area, and what do you wish you had spent more time doing?

_____

_____

_____

_____

_____

_____

Last, are your relationships with others positive and rewarding? What do you gain from the primary relationships in your life? What do you give to those people you are closest to? What primary need do you have that you feel is not getting met in these relationships?

_____

_____

_____

_____

_____

_____

Our need for interpersonal relationships and what brings fulfillment in them changes throughout our life span. What we needed socially at nineteen may not be the same as what we need at fifty-one. This is true regarding both social outlets and friendships, as well as our intimate partners. Creating a wellness plan is something that is progressive; it changes over time based on where we are in our lives. You may crave fewer social opportunities when you are married, raising young children, and building a career than when you are experiencing an empty nest, have an established career, and feel you have more time for yourself and others.

The key to creating social wellness lies within our ability to communicate well with others. What is your communication style? Do you tend to say whatever is on your mind, regardless of its impact? Do you tend to hold your thoughts and feelings in, so as not to be misunderstood? Do you communicate your needs openly, or do you feel the needs of others are more important than your own? Take a few minutes and write down those things you would like the people you care about to know about you that they may not. Include your deepest desires and dreams, what you would attempt if you had no restrictions, no fears. Include whether you feel significant or insignificant to others in your life—and why.

_____

_____

_____

_____

_____

_____

_____

Some people experience anxiety around social situations. Sometimes it occurs when having a new experience or maybe when it involves going somewhere alone. What keeps you from an experience that you may want to have? Do you have a fear of what others may think of you if you are taking a class in something new? Do you feel uncomfortable attending an event alone? Are you fearful of being yourself in new relationships and feel you have to adapt to another person's expectations? Take a few minutes and write down what obstacles currently exist around social relationships for you.

_____

_____

_____

_____

_____

_____

_____

Okay, so what showed up for you? What obstacles do you see? Now I want you to look at how to overcome those obstacles. Let's start with feeling uncomfortable attending a class or event alone. What we typically do is ask ourselves a series of questions that increase our anxiety, such as "What if everyone else there knows what they're doing and I don't?" or "What if everyone is there with someone and I just stand out?" or "What if I get there and I don't like it?" So, what do these questions do? They ask your brain to brainstorm all the ways this could happen, therefore making the obstacles appear even bigger.

Think about it. Your brain is a giant computer. It will search for answers based on what you ask, just like Google. If you ask, "Why do I feel anxious?" it will generate several reasons why you should feel anxious, in turn, making you more anxious. What if you change the question? Let's say we ask, "What can I do to feel more comfortable going to this class?" or maybe "What am I looking forward to in attending this event?" What types of answers will your brain generate for you? It will come up with all the wonderful reasons why you should go and how fabulous it will be. So, let's try this on the obstacles you came up with above.

Write down any anxiety you feel around social situations, any dread, any obstacle that you see and write a question that seeks a solution.

_____

_____

_____

_____

_____

_____

_____

Practice this in any area in which you find that you are hesitant or see an obstacle in your life. It all starts with being aware of what we are thinking and asking and then changing it to something that is productive and useful.

Intimate Relationships

Let's spend a little time on our intimate relationships, as the quality of our lives is often in direct proportion to the quality of our relationships. There are six vital ingredients to a healthy relationship:

1. Taking responsibility for communicating your needs and desires to your partner

2. Becoming intentional in your interactions

3. Learning to value your partner's needs and wishes as highly as you value your own

4. Searching within yourself for the strengths and abilities you are lacking and recognizing those in your partner—as we are typically attracted to a partner who has what we lack

5. Becoming more aware of your drive to be loved, whole, and united

6. Accepting that the way to have a good marriage is to be a good partner

How would you want to be described by your partner? What type of husband, wife, girlfriend, boyfriend do you want to be? So often, we get caught up in what the other person is or is not doing, and we change who we are in relationship to them. This is the first mistake couples often make. So, let's take a moment and write down three words that you would like to describe yourself in the relationship (i.e., loving, honest, and affectionate). Okay, here goes …

1)

2)

3)

Why is it important to you to be these things? What does it say about you as a person? What do they bring to your relationship, and how do you live them out day-to-day? See, often we get caught up in the game of "I would be more affectionate if only he would …". Our interactions become based on what our partner is doing or not doing rather than on who we are as a person. I know it's hard to be loving when the person comes home angry from work every day and puts up an emotional wall. This is where asking the right question comes back into play. Ask yourself, "What can I do to be more loving today?" Or better yet, ask your partner, "What can I do to help you today?" Oftentimes, couples come into counseling wanting to change the other person, when in reality you have to start with yourself.

Start each new day by asking yourself, "How can I be more (fill in the blanks with the three words you chose to describe yourself) today?" Or end your day with "Was I (fill in the blanks) today?" If the answer is no, decide what you can do to be more aligned with who you are tomorrow.

Chapter 4

Emotional Wellness

What Is Emotional Wellness?

Frustration, anger, resentment, jealousy, depression, anxiety—compare these to joy, passion, excitement, and peace. We define our lives by our emotions on a daily basis. Are we having a good day or a bad day, and what does each entail? Often, what we do, how we react, and what we attempt is based on how we feel, not on our talents, desires, and abilities. We find that if events occurring around us are positive, we feel good, and if events occur that we don't like, we are depressed, unhappy, or anxious. Sometimes we attempt to just stop feeling by using alcohol or drugs or just going to sleep and calling it a day.

In this section, we are going to look at how your thoughts, emotions, and behaviors are all connected. Take a couple moments and answer the following questions:

1) When was the last time you felt frustrated? What was occurring? What did you tell yourself about what was occurring, and how did you react?

_____

_____

_____

_____

_____

_____

2) When was the last time you felt excited? What was occurring? What did you tell yourself about what was occurring, and how did you react?

_____

_____

_____

_____

_____

_____

Our feelings are not the result of events that happen to us but rather our interpretation and what we tell ourselves about the event. There will be more about this to follow.

Understanding Your Emotions

What are emotions? Emotions are your body's way of communicating with you, when something is great or when something needs attention. Rather than tuning into what our emotions are telling us, we let our emotions determine our behaviors and thoughts.

For instance, if you have an opportunity to do something you have never done before, you will feel *anxiety*. So, how do you define what anxiety is? To one person, it could be excitement about a new opportunity and a reminder that you need to prepare to be successful. This same feeling to someone else may mean it's too dangerous, too risky; you have the potential to fail, and it's to be avoided. Which is right? Whichever one you want to be right. Often, we have to examine our vocabulary, as we all tend to group things into categories. Anxiety could mean excitement, and depression could mean you need to make a change. Let's start by identifying positive emotions that you feel on a weekly basis. List those emotions you have experienced recently.

_____   _____

_____   _____

Next, write what these emotions felt like in your body. Did you experience a rush of energy? Did you feel light and free? Did your breathing slow down or speed up? Did your posture change? If you need to, stop and imagine the last time you felt like this and bring it back up now to really pay attention to your body in that moment. How do you interact with others? If this is too difficult, skip it and come back the next time one of these emotions arise.

_____

_____

_____

_____

_____

_____

Last, I want you to pay attention to the thoughts that you have when you have this emotion. What do you tell yourself?

_____

_____

_____

_____

_____

Now let's do the same exercise looking at any emotions you experienced in the past week that would be considered negative. Write them down.

_____   _____

_____   _____

Next, write what these emotions felt like in your body. Did you experience a rush of a quickening heart rate or a sense of heaviness? Did your breathing slow down or speed up? Did your posture change? If you need to, stop and imagine the last time you felt like this and bring it back up now to really pay attention to your body in that moment. How do you interact with others? If this is too difficult, skip it and come back the next time one of these emotions arise.

_____
_____
_____
_____
_____
_____

Last, I want you to think about the thoughts that you had when you experienced this emotion. What did you tell yourself?

_____
_____
_____
_____
_____
_____
_____

Do you see the connection between what you feel, what you think, and how you act? It seems pretty basic, I know, but this is a crucial component of learning how to regulate your emotions. No emotion is to be avoided, as they all have meaning in our lives. What you need to learn to do is identify the emotion, identify the origin of the emotion and its meaning, and then identify the behavior and thought that accompanies it.

Let's go through an example. Its Friday at 5:30 p.m., and you are planning on going out with friends tonight. You have been excited all week. At 6:15 p.m., you receive a text stating the plans have changed and they aren't going to be able to make it. How do you feel? Let's assume you are pretty good at regulating your emotions. You may identify feeling disappointed due to having looked forward to your plans for the evening. Your thought might be, That stinks. I was really looking forward to tonight. I guess I need to come up with something else to do. Your behavior will be cooking an easy dinner at home and renting a movie to watch. Okay, the same scenario with someone who is less good at emotional regulation may look like this: How do you feel? Depressed because I have nothing to do tonight; my friends canceled on me. Your thoughts might be, I can't ever count on anyone. I hate being alone, and now I am going to have a miserable night. What behavior would follow? Probably going home, bingeing on unhealthy foods, and going to bed. What is the difference here? The same scenario can have two—if not infinitely more—outcomes, depending on your thoughts, emotions, and belief.

The last of the human freedoms is to choose one's
attitude in any given set of circumstances.
—Viktor E. Frankl

Changing How You Feel

One of the things that I find helpful and use often in therapy is a cognitive behavioral framework for helping you look at events and your response to them. Below is a framework you can use to begin to identify what you may be doing that has you stuck. Start by completing the framework with your initial response and then go back and change the "thought" portion and see how the remaining items change along with it.

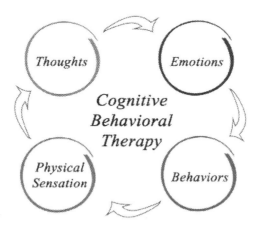

This is one tool to enhance your awareness of how your thoughts, emotions, and body are all tied together in everything that you experience.

Meditation

Sometimes you have to remind your body how it feels to feel gratitude, love, and enjoyment. I would encourage you to start a daily practice of meditation as another way to enhance your emotional well-being. Although I won't go into all the ways that the body stores your emotions and the consequences it has on your health, I do want to give you some simple ways to begin to teach your body to store positive emotions. If you are new to meditation, it can be challenging at first. Be patient with yourself and remember that anything new takes a while to accomplish. The following is a simple mantra-based meditation you can do on your own.

To start, you want to find a quiet location where you are unlikely to be disturbed for fifteen to twenty minutes. Sit in a comfortable position with your hands resting gently in your lap and palms facing up. Close your eyes and focus your attention on your breath, breathing in through your nose and out through your mouth. As you notice yourself starting to relax, silently introduce the mantra "So Hum," silently in your mind saying "So" on the inhale and "Hum" on the exhale. Let this mantra flow effortlessly, bringing your focus to it when you find your mind wandering to thoughts, outside noises, and so on. When done, release the mantra and slowly open your eyes. As you practice this basic meditation, you will begin recognizing gaps between your thoughts; this is where you can remain quiet or introduce thoughts or intentions, such as "I feel gratitude in my life" or "I feel joy in all that I do" or any other phrase that feels rights for you.

Journaling

Journaling is another great way to help you sort out your emotions and thoughts. Journaling can be a freeing exercise and should encompass your goals, your progress, your joys, and your struggles. As you naturally allow your thoughts to flow, you will find creative solutions to problems, have a clearer perspective on things, and recognize triumphs and joys that you may have forgotten. In addition, journaling is shown to assist in achieving your goals, improve mindfulness, enhance self-discipline, improve creativity, and aid in healing. Take out a notebook and a pen and start writing about anything that comes to mind. In appendix A, I have provided you with thirty days of journaling prompts to help with self-reflection and growth. Feel free to use these if free writing is not for you.

Focusing Your Intentions

Lastly, here is a daily exercise you can do that will aid in focusing your intentions in the morning and reflecting on your day in the evening.

Morning Focus Exercise

I am grateful for:

1. _____

2. _____

3. _____

What would make today great is:

1. _____

2. _____

3. _____

Daily affirmation for today:

Evening Reflection Exercise

Three amazing things that happened today are:

1. _____

2. _____

3. _____

I could have made today even better by:

1. _____

2. _____

3. _____

Chapter 5

Environmental Wellness

What Is Environmental Wellness?

So why am I including environmental wellness in your overall wellness plan? Our environment and how we live within it is a crucial factor in our physical, emotional, and spiritual health. From the ancient Chinese practice of Feng Shui to the focus on green living and decreasing our carbon footprint, there is a great deal of information available about how our environment affects us.

Our recognition of our interdependence with nature is currently being explored more than ever as we are learning how it impacts our physical and emotional health as well as our overall quality of life. Environmental awareness includes recycling, adapting a "leave no trace" mind-set, conservation, spending time in natural surroundings, creating positive workplaces and homes, and enhancing air quality, to name a few. Let's start by taking a look at where you are currently in the area of environmental wellness.

Benefits of Nature

Do you spend time outside daily? What is your favorite activity when outside? Do you notice a change in how you feel after spending time outside?

_____

_____

_____

_____

_____

_____

Spending time outdoors has been shown to improve your emotional health. It allows you to connect with nature, enhancing your experience of spirituality, and can significantly reduce anxiety. There's even something called forest therapy. It involves spending time in forested areas for the purpose of enhancing health, wellness, and happiness. When outside, you also tend to be active, whether it's walking on the beach, taking a hike, or working in the garden. This week, I encourage you to spend a total of at least ninety minutes outside engaging in an activity or even simply sitting and reading. A great side effect of time spent outside is the absorption of vitamin D from exposure to sunlight, which will help the body absorb calcium (one of bone's main building blocks). So, not only is it relaxing, but it can promote your physical health as well.

Identify at least three activities that you can engage in outside. Think outside of your usual area. Is there a local trail you could go explore, a botanical garden you could visit, or an outdoor activity you would like to try?

1) _____

2) _____

3) _____

So, what if you just don't have the opportunity to get outside on a daily basis. Then it's time to bring the outdoors in. This concept is typically heralded by interior designers who are creating a relaxing, nature-inspired space. So, what are the benefits of having plants and flowers indoors? Joey Doherty in his Mindfulness Wellness blog lists the following benefits:

1. Houseplants make you smarter and more creative.

Given that plants increase the amount of oxygen in your home and remove toxins, they improve your concentration, memory, reaction time, and creativity. Experimental studies show that cognitive performance is better in offices with plants, and simply seeing green, leafy plants makes us more creative.

2. Houseplants can provide a sense of connectedness.

It's human nature to crave connection with others. Plants remind us that we are sharing this world with more than just other people and that we are all in it together. Everything on this planet plays a role in the circle of life. Having a plant in your home can serve as a reminder of our connection with the rest of this wonderful world. When we breathe, we take in oxygen and release carbon dioxide. Plants do the opposite, by taking in carbon dioxide and releasing oxygen, making us the perfect team.

3. Houseplants reduce anxiety.

Plants make us feel calm. Looking at a living, green plant brings a relaxing sensation that looking at a TV or computer screen will never match. In fact, studies have shown that patients in hospital rooms with plants report that they feel less anxious compared to patients in rooms without plants.

4. Houseplants give us a sense of purpose.

Taking care of a plant gives us a sense of purpose. Being the reason a living thing is alive and well is beautiful and empowering.

5. Houseplants can help you recreate yourself.

When you're ready to make some loving changes in your life to get closer to your best self, consider buying a houseplant when you make those changes. The moment you began loving yourself more by improving your lifestyle can be symbolized by that wonderful plant. Every time you look at it, you'll be reminded of why you made those changes and how far you've come!

6. Houseplants purify the air of toxins.

In today's modern world, we are exposed to a number of toxins that deplete our brain health, even in our own homes. The EPA has even stated that indoor air pollution is one of the greatest risks to our health. Cleaning supplies, candles, beauty products, cookware, smoke, and more release neurotoxins into our air, which can harm our brains. All plants clean the air, but NASA has shown that certain plants are especially effective.

7. Houseplants speed up the healing process.

Studies have shown that patients recover more quickly from surgery when their hospital rooms have plants and flowers in them. Patients with plants in their room had lower blood pressure, lower ratings of pain, less anxiety, and less fatigue than patients without plants in their room.

8. Houseplants teach us to slow down.

Caring for houseplants requires patience. Shortcuts don't work with plants, just like they don't work with our own health. When a plant is unwell with shriveled brown leaves, we can't just paint the leaves green and call it a day. Instead, we ought to look at the whole picture, taking our time and getting to know what amount of sunlight and water the plant needs to thrive. Maybe once we learn how to take care of our houseplants more holistically, we will start taking care of ourselves more holistically, instead of opting for quick fixes.

Our brains are chronically stressed because we're stimulated all the time these days. Taking time out of your day to slowly water a houseplant and carefully check its leaves to see how its feeling, gives your brain a needed break from the constant stimulation.

9. Houseplants reduce the effects of stress.

A research study demonstrated that geraniums helped individuals recover faster and more completely from high-stress situations. If you consider yourself chronically stressed, something kind you could do for yourself is to make your most stressful environments more calming, by putting houseplants in those rooms.

10. Houseplants reduce your number of sick days.

Being around plants means you are constantly exposed to natural medicine. A researcher has discovered an airborne antifungal and antibacterial compound called phytoncides, which plants emit and we are able to benefit from if we are near them.

11. Houseplants improve your sleep.

Quality sleep is crucial for psychological health. There are several reasons indoor plants improve sleep. Houseplants naturally purify the air in your home, so having a few in your bedroom will improve the quality and quantity of your sleep. Simply looking at plants make us feel calmer and less stressed, which will put us in the right mind-set before going to bed. To get the most out of them, choose a plant for your bedroom that continues to release oxygen even at night (most plants do not), such as a snake plant.

Identify at least two rooms in your home where you can add plants or fresh cut flowers. If you don't have a green thumb, start with succulents or ferns, which are easier to care for than other plants.

Decluttering

Another focus of environmental wellness is simplification. By simplifying your living space, you can create a home that is relaxing and peaceful. Andrew Weil, MD, writes that "a home should be a soothing, healing sanctuary and not a source of chemical and emotional stress." Through years of living, we tend to accumulate things that are no longer needed or used, yet we are hesitant to get rid of them. What have you not used in the past year? Is there someone in your community who could benefit from it? Take time to go look through your home, going through closets and drawers and get rid of what no longer serves you. Cleaning out of old, unused, or worn items is cleansing not only for your home but for your soul as well. The act of decluttering has a way of generating fresh energy and creating both mental and physical space, which improves focus and clarity. Clutter and unattended items have been shown to increase your general level of anxiety by adding stress and nagging thoughts of what still needs to be done.

Recognize that clutter may also symbolize other areas of your life you are leaving unattended. Perhaps you are working so many hours that you don't have time to devote attention to yourself or your home. Or perhaps the disorganization and clutter in your home reflect a low level of depression you have been experiencing. Take time to answer the following questions:

1. What have I been neglecting in my life?

    _____
    _____
    _____
    _____

2. What would I need my home to look like in order for it to feel relaxing and peaceful?

    _____
    _____
    _____
    _____

3. What keeps me from staying organized and creating a restful home?

    _____
    _____
    _____
    _____

4. Why do I hold on to items that no longer serve a purpose in my life? What would it mean if I were to discard them?

    _____
    _____
    _____
    _____

So, starting today, decide to go through room by room or drawer by drawer and slowly begin the process of letting go—letting go of unneeded items, letting go of the past that no longer serves you, and creating new space for things that excite you and reflect who you are today.

General Environmental Health

Environmental wellness also includes general care for the earth on which we live and becoming more aware of the impact we have on the planet. I'd like for you to take a few minutes to see where you are regarding conservation, recycling, and eliminating toxins from your environment.

What areas do you currently focus on regarding caring for your environment both in your home and the planet as a whole?

_____

_____

_____

_____

_____

_____

What areas are important to you and why?

_____

_____

_____

_____

_____

_____

Now let's look at areas where you can have an impact. Following each area is a space to allow you to grade yourself on how you are in this area and to note what you would like to do to improve.

1. **Conserving energy.** One of the best ways to conserve electricity is by switching off all the lights and appliances when not in use. You can wash your clothes in a washing machine using both warm and cold water instead of using hot water.

    _____

    _____

    _____

    _____

2. **Drive your car less.** When able, walk or ride your bike. Do you have places that you drive to that would actually be quicker to just walk? If you live in a city or rural area, you can often use other modes of transportation to get around.

_____

_____

_____

_____

3. **Reduce usage of chemicals and pesticides.** It is always advisable to eliminate household chemicals and pesticides that directly pollute the green environment. There are so many environmentally friendly products on the market now that you can easily purchase products that are healthier for you and your family. If you want to go more old school, you can make your own solutions for cleaning using distilled vinegar, lemon, and baking soda.

_____

_____

_____

_____

4. **Recycle the waste products.** Many waste products like glass, plastics, aluminum, cardboard, and paper can be recycled instead of been disposed of in the trash. You can also use reusable towels and bags rather than using disposable ones.

_____

_____

_____

_____

5. **Reduce carbon footprints.** There are many ways to cut back carbon footprints causing excess air pollution. You can lower the temperature of your water heater, wash dishes manually instead of using a dishwasher, reduce the use of air conditioner and furnace, or buy energy-efficient lights to lower the energy consumption level.

_____

_____

_____

_____

6. **Grow or purchase your food locally.** Growing or purchasing locally grown foods aids in reducing the overall commercial transportation of food items that require pesticides and preservatives to preserve them. Eating locally sourced food is also shown to be healthier.

_____

_____

_____

_____

Environmental wellness is a key part of your wellness in other areas, primarily emotionally and physically. By reducing use, removing toxins, simplifying, and adding plants to your space, you will create a healthier, more relaxing and healing environment. By enjoying nature and spending time outside, you will naturally be more active, sleep better, and feel more spiritually connected.

Chapter 6

Spiritual Wellness

EVERY HEART
HAS A PURPOSE

What Is Spiritual Wellness?

Spirituality consists of how you interpret your world, organize your day-to-day living, and assess your way of life. It's your belief about what life is about, how people should engage one another, and what you prioritize in life. Spirituality is the way that you find meaning, hope, comfort, and inner peace.

Eckhart Tolle in his book *The Power of Now* states that through spirituality you realize "that all the things that truly matter—beauty, love, creativity, joy, inner peace—arise from beyond the mind." Developing your spirituality has positive effects on your health. For years, the connection between spirituality and health and healing has been studied. This research shows that healing and your overall health are enhanced by utilizing a spiritual practice.

Some of the practices that aid in developing spiritual awareness include the following

- the development of a deep appreciation for the natural forces that exist all around you
- meditation and prayer
- religious affiliation
- taking the time for exploring and enjoying the outdoors
- watching a sunrise or sunset
- outdoor activities
- gratitude

If you are starting a spiritual practice, it can often be helpful to start by clarifying your values and beliefs. Let's start by identifying what you want your life to stand for, how you want to engage with others, and what principles you want to guide your life. Living by your values reduces anxiety and depression and enhances your general sense of well-being.

Values

Exercise 1: Look at the following list of values and circle up to ten that you hold most important.

Adventure	Achievement	Authenticity
Compassion	Conformity	Connection
Contribution	Courage	Creativity

Equality	Excitement	Flexibility
Freedom	Friendliness	Forgiveness
Generosity	Gratitude	Health
Humor	Humility	Independence
Integrity	Justice	Kindness
Mindfulness	Order	Patience
Persistence	Power	Reciprocity
Respect	Self-Awareness	Self-Care
Self-Development	Spirituality	Trust

Now, try to narrow this list down by half, to the top five values that you hold, and list them here.

_____ _____ _____ _____ _____

Exercise 2: Let's apply these values to three specific areas of your life—relationships, social interactions, and work. This exercise will help you to take a closer look at where you are living your values and where this is a struggle for you. For each area identified below, list each of the values you selected and take a few minutes to identify how you practice this value in your life and what struggles you have found in living this value.

1. Relationships:

My identified values are:

1) _____

How I practice this value in this area of my life:

_____
_____
_____
_____

Where I struggle practicing this value in this area of my life:

_____
_____
_____
_____

2) _____

    How I practice this value in this area of my life:

_____
_____
_____
_____

    Where I struggle practicing this value in this area of my life:

_____
_____
_____
_____

3) _____

    How I practice this value in this area of my life:

_____
_____
_____
_____

    Where I struggle practicing this value in this area of my life:

_____
_____
_____
_____

4) _____

    How I practice this value in this area of my life:

_____
_____
_____
_____

Where I struggle practicing this value in this area of my life:

_____
_____
_____
_____

5) _____

How I practice this value in this area of my life:

_____
_____
_____
_____

Where I struggle practicing this value in this area of my life:

_____
_____
_____
_____

2. Work

My identified values are:

1) _____

How I practice this value in this area of my life:

_____
_____
_____
_____

Where I struggle practicing this value in this area of my life:

_____
_____
_____
_____

2) _____

How I practice this value in this area of my life:

_____

_____

_____

_____

Where I struggle practicing this value in this area of my life:

_____

_____

_____

_____

3) _____

How I practice this value in this area of my life:

_____

_____

_____

_____

Where I struggle practicing this value in this area of my life:

_____

_____

_____

_____

4) _____

How I practice this value in this area of my life:

_____

_____

_____

_____

Where I struggle practicing this value in this area of my life:

_____
_____
_____
_____

5) _____

How I practice this value in this area of my life:

_____
_____
_____
_____

Where I struggle practicing this value in this area of my life:

_____
_____
_____
_____

3. Social/Leisure Time

My identified values are:

1) _____

How I practice this value in this area of my life:

_____
_____
_____
_____

Where I struggle practicing this value in this area of my life:

_____
_____
_____
_____

2) _____

How I practice this value in this area of my life:

_____
_____
_____
_____

Where I struggle practicing this value in this area of my life:

_____
_____
_____
_____

3) _____

How I practice this value in this area of my life:

_____
_____
_____
_____

Where I struggle practicing this value in this area of my life:

_____
_____
_____
_____

4) _____

How I practice this value in this area of my life:

_____
_____
_____
_____

Where I struggle practicing this value in this area of my life:

_____

_____

_____

_____

5) _____

How I practice this value in this area of my life:

_____

_____

_____

_____

Where I struggle practicing this value in this area of my life:

_____

_____

_____

_____

Great. Now let's begin to look at where you are successful in living your values and how to improve where you have identified struggles. Living your values is based on self-awareness and mindfulness practices. You have to begin to be mindful of your values and aware of when you are not acting in accordance with them. I would challenge you to use the next two weeks to do a daily reflection that is similar to this exercise you just completed. At the end of each day, take a few minutes to again look at your identified values and evaluate how you did living by them. You may find that something you have identified as a value is not as important to you as you thought. That's fine. Just go back to the original list and pick another of the original ten. I have included a sheet for the daily reflection in appendix B.

Meditation

A daily meditation practice has been shown to be useful in reducing stress, controlling anxiety, promoting overall emotional health, creating a spiritual connection, and fighting age-related illness. Developing a meditation practice is encouraged, whether it's through silent meditation, guided meditation, or primordial sound meditation, to name just a few.

Here are some of the more common types of meditation.

1. Loving-kindness meditation

Loving-kindness meditation is also known as Metta meditation. Its goal is to develop an attitude of love and kindness. While breathing deeply, you open your mind to the receiving loving-kindness and send messages of loving-kindness to your loved ones, your community, or the world in general. It is designed to promote feelings of love and compassion. This type of meditation can be especially helpful for those affected by anger, frustration, resentment, or interpersonal conflict. The benefits of this type of meditation are that it can increase positive emotions while decreasing depression and anxiety.

2. Progressive relaxation

Progressive relaxation meditation is also known as scan meditation. The focus is on scanning your body for areas of tension, with the goal of noticing tension and allowing it to release. When practicing this type of meditation, you start at one end of the body and work your way through, perhaps starting at your feet and working up toward the crown of your head.

Progressive relaxation can help to promote generalized feelings of calmness and relaxation and has been shown to help with relieving pain. Because it slowly and steadily relaxes the body, it can also be effective in promoting improved sleep.

3. Mindfulness meditation

Mindfulness is a form of meditation that has recently become more popular. It focuses on remaining in the present moment. It encourages awareness of your surroundings and a lack of judgment. It involves allowing thoughts and feelings to ebb and flow without the need to reflect on them.

A form of mindfulness is involved in most kinds of meditation. Breath awareness encourages practitioners to be aware of their breathing, while progressive relaxation draws attention to areas of tension in the body. Mindfulness can be useful in improving focus and memory, decreasing impulsivity, and controlling emotional reactions.

4. Breath awareness meditation

Breath awareness is a type of mindful meditation that encourages mindful breathing. In breathing meditation, the focus is on the slow, deliberate exhale and inhale of the breath. By centering your focus on your breathing, you are able to refocus when thoughts enter your mind. Breath awareness meditation can help with reducing anxiety, improving concentration, creating a spiritual center, and enhancing your emotional response.

5. Zen meditation

Zen meditation is a form of meditation that is often part of a Buddhist practice. Zen practitioners often study under a teacher due to the specific steps and postures it involves. The goal of this type of meditation is similar to mindfulness, with the focus on breathing and observing your thoughts without judgment. This type of meditation is sometimes preferred if you are seeking relaxation and enhanced spirituality.

6. Transcendental meditation

Transcendental meditation is a spiritual form of meditation with a goal of transcending above your current state of being. It is most often focused on a mantra, which is determined by a number of factors. For instance, primordial sound meditation is based upon a specific sound based on the date and time of your birth. Practicing this type of meditation often leads to new spiritual experiences and increased mindfulness.

For many of these, you can find guided meditations online to help you get started. There are also apps available such as Headspace that can be downloaded. You can also check your community for meditation classes, which are sometimes held separate or as part of a mindfulness or yoga class.

Identify at least two types of meditation that you are interested in trying:

1) _____

2) _____

One important note regarding meditation is that it's a practice that one has to develop. It is recommended that in developing a meditation practice, you dedicate at least ten minutes a day every day in order to feel the benefits.

Spirituality and Nature

I personally find that a connection to nature can be powerful, whether it's hiking in the woods, sitting on the beach, or kayaking down a river. By being outdoors, you are able to see the universe at work and the interdependent relationships all around you. Meditation and prayer can be even more powerful when done in a natural environment. Oftentimes, as children, we spend time outside walking, running, playing, and exploring. How often do you spend time outside on a weekly basis? What would you like to do more of that involves getting outdoors? Would you like to take up a sport, take more walks on the beach, or simply sit outside at the end of the day and listen to the sounds around you? I encourage you to make time daily to be outside.

Get friendly with the elements. Whether that means you take a swim in the ocean or go camping in the forest, simply put, get into nature. Learn about the plants and flowers that are native to your area. Be curious about the changes in weather and the difference in how you feel and the response by the birds and other animals. On a sunny morning, do you hear the birds out chirping earlier? After a spring rain, do you notice flowers beginning to bloom?

Go barefoot. Our skin breathes and absorbs vitamins and minerals from the earth. If you go barefoot on the beach, for example, the negative ions from the natural salts in the sand and sea are said to have magnificent healing effects on the body. If you're not near the sand, simply digging your feet into the dirt or soil can be of benefit. In short, let the skin of your feet touch the earth, whether it's on the grass, soil, or sand.

Change your mind state. Realize that nature is not just something on the outside in your environment but a part of your very being. The same vitamins and minerals in nature are the very substance from which your bones and body are built. The oxygen that we breathe is from a symbiotic relationship between humans and trees, in which we both provide the necessary element for one another to live and thrive.

Identify six outdoor activities available to you that you can engage in on a weekly basis. They can be as simple as going outside each morning and enjoying your coffee or as ambitious as including an outdoor running or bike-riding regimen throughout the week. You decide what is right for you. I want you to choose six so that you will stretch your imagination a little and think outside of your typical comfort zone.

My six outdoor activities can include:

1)_____

2)_____

3)_____

4)_____

5)_____

6)_____

I will begin building these into my life on this date: _____. I will spend time outdoors for at least _____ minutes, _____ days a week.

Building a Community

Finding a spiritual community can be powerful as you join in fellowship with others who are on a path to increase connection to God and the universe. I frequently hear that people are searching for this in their life. Often, they are looking for a church that is a good fit for them. A spiritual community offers opportunities not only for spiritual growth but to connect on a social level as well. Go to area churches and find one in which you feel welcomed and at peace when attending. Most churches offer study groups, activities, and areas in which you can serve in your community. These are all benefits of being part of a spiritual community.

Serving others is a crucial component in developing spiritual growth. Time and again, I hear others talk about what they get out of serving others. This may be in the form of going on a mission trip, helping a family in your community, leading a Sunday school class, or serving in a soup kitchen. I encourage you to develop a sense of servitude in your life, finding a way that you can give back to your community. Part of your spiritual development is recognition of your spiritual connection to other people.

If you have been part of a spiritual community in the past and have fallen away, take a few minutes to recall the positive aspects you received from that. How did it help keep you centered and focused on a weekly basis on what's important in your life? Was there a sense of acceptance and being a part of something bigger than yourself? Write about that experience below. If you have never been part of a spiritual community, write your goals regarding what you would like to find and how you will begin your search.

_____

_____

_____

_____

_____

Gratitude

Starting every day with a time of gratitude not only enhances your connection with spirit but also helps shift you into a positive mind-set. By now, we have all heard of the power of attraction. Not only recognizing but also feeling gratitude in your life helps generate the recognition of even more positive events and feelings. I have had numerous people tell me that they practice gratitude, but it doesn't help. When I explore this further, I typically find that they are doing a mental exercise rather than a physical one. When I talk about experiencing gratitude, it's not only saying what it is you are grateful for but *feeling* grateful in your body—allowing yourself to appreciate and feel what it is you are grateful for in your life. For example, maybe you are grateful for your children. As you say this out loud, imagine how it feels to see excitement on their faces or to feel their hugs when you arrive home each day. It is only through truly allowing yourself to feel grateful that a practice of gratitude can improve your life. Let's try it now. Write down three things you are truly grateful for in your life:

1)_____

2)_____

3)_____

Now take a few minutes and allow yourself to *feel* truly grateful for each of these. What do you notice as you allow yourself to feel gratitude, to experience the miracles that you have in your life?

Some people prefer to end their day with this practice. By ending the day with thoughts of things you are grateful for, your perspective begins to shift, and you realize that each day really is wonderful and full of gifts. All you have to do is take the time to appreciate them and open space up for so many more wonderful things to enter your life. Others prefer to start their day with the practice of gratitude, which opens your mind to the possibility of new and exciting things coming your way throughout the day. It eliminates any sense of dread you may feel as you move forward and helps you start your day with a positive outlook.

The Hasidic rabbi Zuscha was asked on his deathbed what he thought the kingdom of God would be like. He replied, "I don't know. But one thing I do know. When I get there, I am not going to be asked, 'Why weren't you Moses? Why weren't you David?' I am only going to be asked, 'Why weren't you Zuscha? Why weren't you fully you?'"

Chapter F

Financial Wellness

What Is Financial Wellness?

Financial wellness is knowing what your income and debts are and having a plan for how you spend your money. Money problems affect all areas of your life. They can cause issues in marriages and within families as well as cause emotional stress and health problems. I want you to not only feel in control of your money but be able to create a plan for yourself that ensures you are not living paycheck to paycheck and feel confident that you will be able to meet your own basic needs. Abraham Maslow created a hierarchy of needs, which states that we achieve our full potential by moving from basic needs to self-actualization. Our first level of needs include the need for food, water, shelter, and clothing. When we struggle to meet our basic needs, it impacts all areas of our growth.

Unfortunately, most of us live above our means. We spend money in excess of what we make by taking out loans, financing what we buy, and buying more than we need. In order to achieve financial success, you have to learn to live below your means. This is a hard concept for most of us to live by. We tend to justify why we need more, bigger, and better. As we move forward, you will take a look at not only where you are but where you ultimately would like to be and the shift in mind-set it will take to get there. Let's start by identifying the steps to financial wellness.

Steps to Creating Financial Wellness

Step 1: Identify Your Starting Point

You have to start by identifying and acknowledging where you are at this moment. What is your income, what are your debts, and what are your monthly expenses? One of the biggest mistakes you can make is to ignore where you are currently, yet this is what a lot of people do. They don't want to take a real look at what they owe or accept the fact that they have more month than they do money. Use this short exercise to get a solid look at your starting point.

Monthly Income:
Source: _____

Amount: _____

Source: _____

Amount: _____

Source: _____

Amount: _____
Total: _____

Monthly Expenses:
Rent/Mortgage: _____
Utilities: _____
Insurances: _____
Car Payment: _____
Childcare Expenses: _____
Cable and Phone: _____
Credit Card Payments: _____
Loans: _____
Other: _____
                                                    Total: _____

Total Debts:
Mortgage: _____
Car Loans: _____
Credit Cards: _____
Student Loans: _____
Personal Loans: _____
Debts Owed to Friends/Family: _____
                                                    Total: _____

Total Assets:
Savings Account Balances: _____
Checking Account Balances: _____
Retirement Funds: _____
Savings Bonds: _____
Other Savings: _____
                                                    Total: _____

What did you learn by doing this exercise? Are you surprised by what you see, or are you aware of your current financial situation? In the space below, write what you would like to change regarding your current financial situation, and if you are in a relationship where you share finances, what you would need from your spouse in order to move forward.

_____
_____
_____
_____
_____
_____
_____

Step 2: Create a Vision

Now let's create a vision for your finances. What does being *financially stable* mean to you? What would you have saved as a nest egg? How much would you be making monthly, and how would you be earning your money? What would you be saving for monthly—retirement, your children's education, vacations, or a down payment for a home? How would you feel when it came to your finances? Take a few minutes and write down what comes to mind for each of these. Try not to think from a place of scarcity, such as "Right now, I'd just like to not be behind on my rent," but from a place of abundance. What is your ultimate vision—not your short term. We will get to that later.

_____

_____

_____

_____

_____

_____

_____

_____

Step 3: Develop a Budget

Creating a budget that you can live by, modify, and get direction from is a key component of financial wellness. There are so many budgeting tools out there that I am not going to give you yet another one but rather refer you to a couple that I think are best. It's important when developing a budget that you see it as a tool, something you develop monthly and modify as needed; it grows and changes with you. If you have a partner whom you live with, it's imperative that you create a budget together. This not only enables you to be on the same page financially, which enhances your overall relationship, but also gives you a place to plan together and dream together.

Dave Ramsey in his *Total Money Makeover* provides a budgeting tool that not only separates out all your income and expenses but gives you percentage guidelines for each item, which can be helpful. In addition, he has created budgeting tools for those with salaried paychecks as well as those for people who work on commission or whose pay changes week to week or month to month. There are both downloadable forms for printing and an app available to use. You can find these tools at www.daveramsey.com.

A second resource that can be helpful is through www.crown.org. While this website does have a subscription you can opt into, there are also a ton of free resources available.

The most important thing is to start today to develop your budget, whether you choose one of these resources or choose one of the myriad available.

Step 4: Implementation

Select a start date for your new budget. Please understand that it's a working document, and in the first few months, you will find that you need to budget more or less in certain categories. It will take those first few weeks to know exactly what you do spend and need to spend on items such as food and gas. It's okay if there isn't much leftover after the basic expenses are paid. It means you may have to live a leaner lifestyle while you get yourself to a place where you are free from debt. Yes, it may be painful at first, but by the end, you will be doing your happy dance.

Developing Your Dream

Now it's time for the fun stuff. Part of what will drive you to get more financially sound is the desire to live the way you want. So, take time either on your own or with your partner to begin thinking about what you want and need in your life. Begin dreaming about what you could do if you were financially strong and weren't worried about being able to pay your monthly bills. Maybe you would want to purchase a home, or take more vacations, or learn a new hobby. Spend some time listing those things that you want to do as you move forward in your life toward financial freedom. Think big and think small. It's a list of things you desire to bring into your life. Let's go with your top ten.

1. _____

2. _____

3. _____

4. _____

5. _____

6. _____

7. _____

8. _____

9. _____

10. _____

Great. Now review this as you work through your budget. Maybe some of these will be included in a savings plan, or maybe they will serve as an inspiration to stay on track. Feel free to change and modify them as you want. It's your plan, your dreams, your future. You create it!

Finding the Joy in Giving

We've all heard it's better to give than to receive. Whether you have spent time reflecting on this in the past or not, I want to spend some time with it now. Can you recall a time when you were excited about a gift that you gave to someone? What was it? Who was it for? How did they react when they received it? How did you feel?

_____
_____
_____
_____
_____
_____

There is something inherently rewarding in being able to help others or to give someone something special as a sign of affection, appreciation, or just because. Becoming financially sound means creating more opportunities to give in whatever way is important to you. Some people include tithing in their budget. Others want to provide their children with college that is paid for. Or maybe you have a cause that's close to your heart that you've always wanted to donate to but could never afford. List below those ways that you would want to help others if you had more money than you needed to meet your expenses. How and to whom would you provide help? List five ways that you would practice generosity and why it's important to you.

1. _____

2. _____

3. _____

4. _____

5. _____

I would want to provide assistance to these people, organizations, or causes because:

_____
_____
_____
_____
_____
_____

Creating financial independence is all about follow-through. It's not something you can do for a week or a month and get results. It's about deciding here and now that you will no longer live a life of worry and frustration when it comes to your finances. It's about knowing you can decide what you earn, how you earn it, and—most importantly—how you will spend your money. It's through determination and faith that you will be able to move to the next level in your financial success. So, stop looking at what your neighbors and friends just bought and focus on you. Stop getting caught up in societal-related status symbols or in mistaken beliefs of *needing* things that aren't *needs*. Set your goal and intention for where you want to be one year from now and what you are going to do to get there.

Today's date: _____

One year from now, I will …

_____
_____
_____
_____
_____

In order to get there, I must …

_____

_____

_____

_____

_____

_____

I will start today by …

_____

_____

_____

_____

Creating a Financial Wealth Mind-Set

You may be asking yourself, "If it's really this simple, then why haven't I achieved this already?" Well, here's the most difficult piece of the whole puzzle. It takes time! Which means you have to be in it for the long haul. It requires changing your mind-set from wanting the short-term feel-good gain to the long-term it-feels-fabulous gain. As human beings, most of us have an extremely difficult time putting off our here-and-now wants in order to gain something bigger and better down the road. We self-sabotage by saying, "I deserve to go out to dinner. I have worked so hard all week." Or "I had my best year yet. I deserve to get a new car. Everyone has car loans. What's the big deal?" The answer to all of these is that ultimately you are working against yourself. Crazy, huh? We do this in so many areas of our lives. We have goals, dreams, and plans, and then we get sidetracked by a shiny new object, or we lose traction because we lack the patience and persistence necessary to see it through.

In order to meet your goals of financial prosperity, you have to develop discipline—discipline to stay within your budget, discipline to live below your means, discipline to sit down each month and create a plan that works. So, let's look at the keys to developing discipline in your life.

1) Get clear about what it is you want to accomplish.

2) Be clear about why you want to accomplish these goals.

3) Identify what changes you will need to make to meet your goal.

4) Prioritize your highest goals, such as creating an emergency fund or paying off debt, and create an action plan.

5) Track your progress.

6) Find someone to help keep you accountable, either your partner or a friend.

Congratulations! You are on your way to a newfound sense of peace through financial responsibility and independence.

We must all suffer from one of two pains: the pain
of discipline or the pain of regret. The difference is
discipline weighs ounces while regret weighs tons.
—Jim Rohn

Chapter 8

Occupational Wellness

What Is Occupational Wellness?

Occupational wellness is the ability to optimize the balance between work and personal life, reducing and preventing stress, and striving for satisfaction and meaning in life through work. Whether this is employment that offers compensation or through volunteering, it's about having purpose. You may see work as what you have to do to pay your bills, or you may have found your calling and enjoy what you do but don't know how to have more balance or more financial success. In this section, you will look at the role that work plays in your life and how you keep from letting it become too stressful or carry over into your personal time. At the same time, you will learn how to value the time you put into your work and be more productive and efficient in the process. The Pareto principle states that 80 percent of the results you achieve come from 20 percent of your actions, but more about this later.

Success is not the key to happiness. Happiness is the key to success.
If you love what you are doing, you will be successful.
—Herman Cain

Identifying Your Purpose

So maybe this phrase has been over used, *finding purpose*. There have been books written on it, sermons given, and whole batteries of questionnaires developed. So, why are we starting here? Our role in the workplace has changed a great deal over the past couple decades. It used to be you found a job, worked your way up the ladder, and retired—or maybe you opened a small business and ran it until you retired. This is now the exception rather than the norm. People frequently switch jobs and companies several times throughout their lives. They may have a job with a company or organization and work a side job at the same time. Now you can go to work, work from home, or work remotely from just about anywhere you want to be. You are limited only by your own imagination. So, we start here because our options are now endless. Your vision and what you want to achieve is what matters, not where you live or the advantages or disadvantages you feel you may have had. Oftentimes, people try to identify the one thing that they are meant to do, which adds a lot of pressure. I suggest you look at all the things that you enjoy doing instead. The first exercise you will do involves being able to identify what you are drawn to in your life. Now, not every hobby or interest should become a career, but let's begin to sort out your talents, strengths, and passions.

What comes easy for you? What do friends and family members always say you are good at doing? Oftentimes, the things you are best at are easily dismissed. It may seem too simple and just "part of who I am," so you may not recognize it as a talent.

_____

_____

_____

_____

_____

_____

What can you do with your time and abilities that would be helpful or make a difference, whether through work or volunteering?

_____

_____

_____

_____

_____

_____

What activities or jobs have you engaged in that you enjoyed? What was it about that activity or job that made it fulfilling for you?

_____

_____

_____

_____

_____

_____

Have you ever thought about your dream job? What would it look like? When would you work? Would it involve travel? Would you work from home? What responsibilities would you have?

_____

_____

_____

_____

_____

_____

_____

If you currently work or volunteer, what drew you to it? What do you like, and what do you dislike? How does it fit with the dream job you described above?

_____

_____

_____

_____

_____

_____

Stress and Work

In a survey conducted by the American Psychological Association in 2017, 60 percent of respondents reported they were stressed at work. Another study conducted by the Center for Creative Leadership found that professionals with smartphones engage with work more than seventy hours a week. The added stress most people report along with the long work hours, both on and off the clock, affect health, relationships, and personal use of time.

So, how do you make your work more productive and less stressful? By focusing more on your overall lifestyle. Factors such as sleep, nutrition, exercising, personal connections, time to play, and relaxation all can increase your work productivity, which in turn eliminates stress. Let's look at each of these areas briefly.

1) **Sleep**. On a daily basis, I have clients who state they are having trouble sleeping, whether it's due to restlessness, pain, being unable to tune out their thoughts, or just frequently waking up. I think we have all at one time or another woken up and felt like we had never slept, or perhaps we were more tired than when we went to bed. Here are some tips to help with sleep.

   • Have a nighttime routine. Most people benefit from having a regular routine, which signals the brain that bedtime is coming. It's recommended that you start preparing for bed about an hour before you plan to go to sleep. During this time, you may choose to read, take a shower, spend time with family members, and so on. Use this time to not engage with phones, TVs, or other electronic devices.

- If you find that you tend to have trouble shutting down your thoughts, try journaling before bed. It's a good way to review your day, plan for tomorrow, and process anything that you may be lying in bed thinking about.
- Sleep in a cool, dark room.
- You may find using a relaxation meditation or even listening to meditative sounds, such as a stream, rainstorm, or music, can assist you in falling asleep.
- Eliminate caffeine and beverages an hour before bedtime.

2) Nutrition. What you eat, when you eat, and where you eat can all impact your energy level throughout the day. Part of being able to manage stress is giving your body what it needs and eliminating those things it doesn't. Here are a few tips to help you make good choices in this area.

- Take a lunch. I know, I know. You are too busy; you don't have time to take lunch. Skipping a midday meal can leave you more tired and less focused and affect your ability to make decisions.
- Step away from your desk when you take lunch. A change of scenery, whether it's going for a drive, sitting in a break room, or taking a walk with a coworker, can do wonders to restore your energy. It's been found that your creativity and problem-solving improves when you step away from your work environment for a period of time.
- When possible, use this time to get outdoors. Being outdoors has been shown to affect mood, blood pressure, and energy levels. When possible, find a natural environment, maybe a local park or a bench outside to sit and relax.
- Be mindful of what you eat. Refined carbs such as breads and sugars are known to temporarily give you an energy lift, only to leave you drained and more tired than when you started. Try to include a lunch that consists of meats, vegetables, fruits, nuts, or dairy.

3) Exercise. It has been well documented in study after study that people who exercise are more productive, have more energy throughout the day, and are better problem solvers. So, whether it's finding time to move before your workday starts or moving frequently throughout the day, this is a key ingredient to feeling less stress and more energetic. Even waiting till the end of the workday can be effective in managing stress and allowing you to transition from work to home.

4) Personal connections. Who we engage with and how often we engage with others can have a profound effect on our energy and mood. Here are some guidelines to make sure your personal connections are restoring your energy and not draining you.

- Avoid workplace gossip. I know, it's not easy, and you probably don't even realize the impact it has on you. Trust me: don't engage in it, and you will notice a difference in no time at all.
- Make sure you are offering positive feedback to those around you. Show others that you appreciate the job they do, thank coworkers for helping out, and feel free to just spread kindness anywhere, anytime. By focusing on the positive, you will experience an improved mood and better problem-solving abilities.
- Make time outside of work hours to connect with the people in your life who you care about. Your personal time should be just that, time free of work distractions where you connect with those you love. This will nourish your soul and rejuvenate your mind.

5) Make time to play. You've heard the line *all work and no play*. So, make time at least weekly to play, whether it's a round of golf, a trip to the playground with your child, or family game night. Make time to interact with others in a manner that allows you to relax, enjoy, and reinvigorate. Yes, even competitive play counts, so join an adult softball league or play tennis with your partner. Playing with people you are close to also enhances your relationships.

6) Relaxation. I frequently hear about people being unable to relax. They have difficulty with downtime, or they feel the need to take care of things that need to be done. Relaxation is about choosing what you want to do over what you have to do. So, for some, relaxation may be working in the yard on their day off, while for others it's lying on the beach and doing absolutely nothing. The benefits to relaxation include lowered blood pressure, improved mood, improved digestion, a reduction in stress hormones, and a noticeable reduction in muscle tension and chronic pain. So, when possible, plan time to relax every day, at the very least every week.

List two areas identified above that you need to make changes in starting now. What will you do different and what do you see as the benefit to creating this change?

_____

_____

_____

_____

_____

_____

_____

Goal Setting

In order to achieve success in your occupation, you must have an idea of where you want to go. Vague goals lead to vague results. What does success look like to you? Is it based on income, flexibility, the satisfaction it brings? In the space below, write how you define *success*. Review your answers in the "Finding Your Purpose" section as you complete this exercise.

_____

_____

_____

_____

_____

_____

Now that you have an idea of what success means to you, let's begin looking at the short-term and long-term goals you have in this area of your life. Below, write a list of your top five goals for where you would like to be when it comes to your career in five years.

_____

_____

_____

_____

_____

_____

_____

Now let's focus on what you would need to do in the next year to move in that direction. Below, list up to ten things you would need to accomplish in the next year to move you closer to your five-year goals. These may be related to actual employment, self-development, or developing new routines or habits.

1.

2.

3.

4.

5.

6.

7.

8.

9.

10.

Keep this list with you so you can review it every day and let it guide your actions. As you go throughout your day, week, and month, ask yourself, "What can I do today to move me closer to my goals?" Review your goals monthly and ensure that your day-to-day habits are in line with what you desire to achieve.

Chapter 9

Intellectual Wellness

What Is Intellectual Wellness?

Intellectual wellness is the openness to new concepts and ideas. It incorporates recognizing your creativity and stimulating mental growth. You are doing well in this area when you strive to expand your knowledge and skills while also discovering the potential for sharing your gifts with others. This can be accomplished through reading and learning, participating in classes and workshops, adopting a new hobby, and traveling to new places.

Throughout this section, I hope to spark your curiosity about *what else*. *What else* you can learn, *what else* can you experience, *what else* can you create, and *what else* you can be? The only limits are those that you place upon yourself.

People with many interests live not only longest, but happiest.
—George Matthew Allen

The Sky's the Limit

Let's start by dreaming a little. Make a list below of the things you would like to learn, places you would like to go, events you want to attend, experiences you would like to have, and subjects that spark your interest. At this point, it doesn't matter how practical it is; we will worry about that later. So, think big!

1. _____

2. _____

3. _____

4. _____

5. _____

6. _____

7. _____

8. _____

9. _____

10. _____

Take a look at what you listed above. Choose the ones that you could start engaging in now. Which ones could you add to your goal list for the next year?

I will start expanding myself intellectually and creatively by:

_____
_____
_____

I plan to start doing these activities by_____ (date).

Creativity

Having a creative outlet is known to reduce stress and anxiety, enhance problem-solving, and improve your sense of general well-being. This is often one of the first things that gets thrown out the door when you get too busy. There are so many opportunities to bring creativity into your life, whether it's through art, cooking, writing, crafts, decorating, or a myriad of other experiences. Creativity is also a crucial part of business development and leads to innovation and productivity. When was the last time you were creative? What were you doing, and how did it feel?

_____
_____
_____
_____
_____
_____

Here are nine ways to help you expand your creativity:

1. Doodle, draw, or paint with no specific outcome in mind. She what you generate and where those first few random marks take you.

2. Read and listen to content outside of your usual comfort zone. Pick a topic you may remotely be interested in but never explored.

3. Do a freewriting exercise where you write about whatever comes to mind—no topic, no editing, just go for it.

4. Go to a restaurant with ethnic foods you have never tried; the atmosphere, the foods, and the culture will all be new to you.

5. Brainstorm with your partner or friend new activities to try, new date night ideas, or new experiences you would like to have together.

6. Run or walk without music or other distractions, letting your mind wander. Both walking and running have been shown to improve creative thinking.

7. Take an art class or participate in a crafting class or activity offered in your community.

8. Take a noncredit class at your local community college in French cuisine, learning a new language or anything that will challenge you.

9. Learn to play a musical instrument, sing, or dance. Music is one of our most basic creative abilities. At the very least, listen to a musical genre that you would not normally listen to and let your mind wander.

10. List here your own creative idea: _____

Identify at least three creative opportunities you will take over the next month.

1) _____

2) _____

3) _____

Connection and Community

I am sure you have heard the saying *you are who you spend your time with*, or some version of it. It's important in creating a sense of intellectual wellness that you spend time in communities and with people who can challenge you, encourage you, and motivate you. With today's online communities, it's easier than ever to make connections with people who share similar interests and ambitions. You can learn from those who have already accomplished a version of what you want to do through reading, participating in mastermind groups, or joining private Facebook communities. You can learn about new subjects through use of your local library, listening to podcasts, online courses, and community college offerings. Oftentimes, there are offerings within your community that you may not be aware of, such as through local art councils, meet-up groups, service organizations, and so on. Look for events, workshops, book clubs, and other groups within your local community that you could take part in.

Learning and Personal Development

The happiest people spend their lifetime gaining new knowledge. Personal development is a process and doesn't end at a certain age but should continue throughout your life. Through personal development, your relationships improve, you are more easily able to adapt, your problem-solving skills become better, and your general sense of self is enhanced. Personal development is about knowing what you are interested in and what your strengths are, then using them to move forward to accomplish your goals. Learning is a key component, whether it's learning more about yourself, about how the human body works and responds to stress, or enhancing your skill set. Often, when we are young, we have to choose an area of interest to pursue, and in doing so, we let go of those areas that intrigued us but were not deemed profitable careers. Do you remember your interests from when you were younger? What were you interested in? What did you read in your spare time? What types of programs did you watch on TV? What did you dream of doing one day? The answer to these questions can help you identify those areas in which you want to continue to grow and learn. Maybe you were interested in space but became an accountant. Do you follow NASA research, study the constellations, and know when meteor events are happening in your area? Or maybe you were interested in acting but became a teacher. Do you attend local theatre productions, or do you try out and participate in local theatre in your area?

In the space below, identify three areas of interest you would like to further develop.

1. _____

2. _____

3. _____

Now, I want you to think about your current career or volunteer projects and identify what you need to learn in order to move to the next level. Maybe you want to enhance your marketing skills, learn more about managing people, or develop your skills regarding doing presentations. Identify three things that you would like to improve on occupationally.

1. _____

2. _____

3. _____

From the two lists you have generated above, I want you to do some goal setting. Looking over the next year, which three of the above six topics do you most want to begin delving into? I want you to identify those three areas as well as the steps you will take to begin learning more. Lastly, I want you to include a plan for when you will begin focusing on this activity and how you will incorporate it into your week.

My top three topics I want to explore more are:

4. _____

   I can learn more about this area by: _____
   _____
   _____

   I plan to begin taking action on (date) _____ by planning time to spend on it when:_____

5. _____

   I can learn more about this area by: _____

   I plan to begin taking action on (date)_____ by planning time to spend on it when: _____

6. _____
   _____
   _____

   I can learn more about this area by:_____
   _____
   _____

I plan to begin taking action on (date) _____ by planning time to spend on it when: _____

Now set a time weekly in your planner to evaluate how you are doing in each of these areas. Each week, you should schedule time to work on each of these three areas in some way. Or maybe you want to break them down and focus on them each individually. In that case, list them in order of importance and spend the next four months focusing on the first topic, the following four months on the second, and the last four months of the year on the last. Either way works; it's whether you would prefer to spread out your interest and learn multiple things at once or focus more on each item. Good luck and go enrich your brain, enhance your learning, and set goals for personal growth that you can meet. As Jim Rohn said, "It's not accomplishing the goal that's important, but who you become along the way."

Month of Journaling

Day 1: Write about how your life would be different if you felt comfortable being yourself at all times. What would you do differently? How would you feel? How would your relationships change?

Day 2: Describe four things you want to accomplish over the next year.

Day 3: Write about something that has caused you emotional pain and what you have done to overcome it. What are the traits that you possess that allow you to be resilient?

Day 4: What areas of your life need the most growth, and how are you working on them?

Day 5: Describe the person you would want to be if you could start from scratch to create a new you.

Day 6: Name one thing you've always wanted to do but haven't. What has prevented you from doing it? What can you do to make it happen?

Day 7: Describe your ideal life. Write about why you're not living it right now. What would you need to do differently in order to make it happen?

Day 8: Write down something you need to let go of and why you have chosen to hold on to it. What would you gain and lose by letting go?

Day 9: Write down three things you would like to improve about yourself, as well as three things that you love about yourself.

Day 10: What would you do if you knew you couldn't fail?

Day 11: What does *success* mean to you?

Day 11: What is something you have always wanted to learn to do? Why haven't you, and what could you do to move in that direction?

Day 12: Who in your life do you wish you had more contact with and why? What can you do to make it happen?

Day 13: Identify one thing that is always on your to-do list but never gets done. What is the pain associated with completing it? What is the benefit?

Day 14: What are two things that you could start doing today that would enhance your relationship?

Day 15: Over the past week, what have you achieved? What have you been disappointed by? Most importantly, what changes will you make over the next seven days to make next week even better?

Day 16: What is your biggest dream? What would it take to achieve it?

Day 17: What do you want most in life, and how do you plan to make it happen? What steps would you need to take over the next week, month, or year to begin moving in that direction?

Day 18: *The reason I haven't followed through in the past is … How I will prevent this from happening again in the future is to …*

Day 19: Write about a belief you have about yourself that keeps you from achieving more. Write alternative beliefs you would like to have that would allow you to move forward.

Day 20: What are two changes you can make to improve your physical health? One should be nutritional, and the other related to movement. What has prevented you from making these changes, and when will you decide to take action?

Day 21: *When thinking about my financial future, I feel …* Identify those things you do well when it comes to managing your money and those things that you can improve on.

Day 22: What is something that you do not like doing or do not feel you do well that you could ask for help with? Who in your life can help you, and how will you go about seeking help?

Day 23: Free journal day. Write about anything that comes to mind. Freewriting is a great way to enhance creativity.

Day 24: Try to meditate today either through silence or with the help of a meditation app and write about your experience.

Day 25: Describe a challenge you are currently facing or one you have overcome. What are you learning about yourself as a result, or what did you learn?

Day 26: Write about a recent disagreement you had with someone you care about from their perspective.

Day 27: What does it mean to you to live a *meaningful* life?

Day 28: If you had three lives, what would you do that you wouldn't do with only one?

Day 29: What people in your life bring out the best in you?

Day 30: *What I have learned about myself in the last thirty days is … What I want to focus on over the next month to create change in my life is … I will do this by …*

Value Reflection Exercise

The top five values by which I live my life are:

1) _____

2) _____

3) _____

4) _____

5) _____

I demonstrated my belief in these values today by:

_____
_____
_____
_____
_____
_____

I struggled in living my values today at these times:

_____
_____
_____
_____
_____
_____

In order to live more in accordance with my values tomorrow, I will:

_____

_____

_____

_____

_____

_____